LINER
NOTES

LINER
NOTES

ANDY MISTER

Station Hill
of Barrytown

Published by Station Hill of Barrytown, the publishing project of the Institute for Publishing Arts, Inc., 120 Station Hill Road, Barrytown, NY 12507, New York, a not-for-profit, tax-exempt organization [501(c)(3)].

Online catalogue: www.stationhill.org
e-mail: publishers@stationhill.org

 This publication is supported in part by grants from the New York State Council on the Arts, a state agency.

Interior and cover design by Yuki Kites.

The author thanks the editors of the following journals where excerpts from *Liner Notes* originally appeared: *Boston Review*, *The Canary*, *Cannibal*, *Five Fingers Review*, */nor*, *Seneca Review*, and *Sink Review*.

Library of Congress Cataloging-in-Publication Data

Mister, Andrew.
  Liner notes / by Andy Mister.
    pages cm
  ISBN 978-1-58177-131-2 (pbk.)
  I. Title.
  PS3613.I8448L56 2013
  811'.6—dc23

                    2013001990

The invention of melody is the supreme mystery of man.
   Claude Levi-Strauss

All art constantly aspires towards the condition of music.
   Walter Pater

Hail, hail rock and roll!
   Chuck Berry

BRIAN WILSON SET out to write a teenage symphony to god and laughter. He called it *Dumb Angel*. During the recording of "Mrs. O'Leary's Cow," Wilson and all of the session musicians wore fireman's caps. In this sense each performer has a conductorial function. *Over and over, the crow cries uncover the cornfield*. Did he burn the tapes because their bad vibes were responsible for a series of fires in Southern California? The lesson of *Smile* is that a record does not have to be heard to create a sound.

I HEARD A car door slam, then birds crashing. The actual duration between sounds is determined at the moment of playing by the performer. Outside my window the city is asleep. Across the street, a man lies in a doorway, sleeping. It's hard not to think about how he could be me. This ginseng tea makes me woozy. If this morning would become summer—not a bird in sight. I tell myself the day is unfolding in words. I tell myself our love is like a pop song. A song in which our love is compared to *Wuthering Heights*: none of the characters are all that likeable.

WHEN I WAS sick, no one knew but the doctors. Now no one knows that I'm well. What risk is there in intending a meaning? What I would do not to feel so jagged. I once heard someone on television singing about that feeling. Did she have you on your knees? I wrote an entire book on the train. In it I defined her as a force, not a person. A moment of affirmation: by accident or effort. Contact is a gift. She is wearing it. Anxiety conferred by the telephone, love's true signature. This feeling I once heard someone singing about.

ERASERHEAD IS ESSENTIALLY a film about a man afraid of becoming a father. During the filming, David Lynch's daughter Jessica was born. I felt sickened by the streaking lights: red, white, yellow, glowing against the glass. And everything was glass. I thought I would break if someone touched me. When I left for work it was still dark out, but the streetlights were off as if they knew nature had made a mistake. How do they know when it's getting dark, I asked. Someone must tell them.

A BOY ON the train asked me why I have a skull on my wrist. I wondered if he meant I was going to die. He asked if it glows in the dark. Then he asked me to buy a candle for five dollars. When we went through the tunnel, I couldn't see anything. I got off at 16th and walked up Valencia. It had been threatening rain when I left, but now the sun was out. Everyone was smiling, which scared me. I kept crossing out words as I went along. The street was lined with blank spaces. I wanted to disappear into them.

As we lay in bed she said, "It's getting dark out," as if I were a machine. An oil stain on asphalt. A spot in the cornea. First the gray then the green washed out of the paragraph, leaving only numbers. I was trying to describe what the air felt like walking to the BART station. Now I only want to explain what it feels like when nothing happens. The weather becomes an occasion. Everyone is out in the middle of it. Today is Lincoln's birthday. The weather becomes the occasion.

Nick Drake delivered the *Pink Moon* tapes to a receptionist at Island Records without a word. Island didn't realize they had the album until after he had left. Shortly after its release Drake checked himself into a psychiatric hospital for five weeks. Thereafter he wrote little music and rarely ventured out except to see friends like John Martyn, who described Drake as "the most withdrawn person I've ever met."

With tightened throats we stare past the impersonal landscape: some trees, a boat cutting a path across the lake. The sky is no wider than a puddle. It's Friday the 13th. I called in sick to work. I watched the water appear and disappear. The water in my eyes. Washed green to gray. Each moment is surrounded by numbers, shining. The weather doesn't start to take shape until spring, then you'll see it all around you. Scattering out from a point. That point is not you. Or me.

ON NOVEMBER 25, 1974, Nick Drake was found dead in his bedroom in his parents' home after taking an overdose of antidepressants. He left no suicide note. "He kept withdrawing and withdrawing until he just disappeared."

WHEN I WAS in junior high a girl I had a crush on told me about a song that actually made you *feel* like you were on heroin when you listened to it. That evening I asked my father if he knew the name of this song.

"'Heroin' is all right," he said. "But you should really listen to 'Sister Ray.'"

MY THROAT TIGHTENED. I crossed MacArthur to the Grand Lake Theatre. It was warmer than it had been in months. Adrift on an ocean of asphalt. In the distance the heat made a mirage floating above the street. But I wasn't going to see a movie, I was going to cash a check.

I READ A profile of Nick Drake in *Entertainment Weekly* while waiting in my psychiatrist's office. There was a resurgence of interest in his music after the song "Pink Moon" was used in a Volkswagen commercial. Now stark folk songs by depressives are used to sell cars. I was secretly rather fond of the commercial. Two young couples drive to a party—in a Volkswagen, I assume. When they arrive, they see a bunch of loud, drunken kids. They turn around and just keep driving. The article was mostly about the commercial, not Drake's life.

ON MAY 10, 1980, Ian Curtis hanged himself in the kitchen of his Macclesfield home. He left a note that read: "At this very moment, I wish I were dead. I can't cope anymore." He was 23 years old. A month earlier, he and his wife—from whom he was separated—had celebrated their daughter's first birthday.

ONCE WHEN I was 13, riding home on the school bus, I drowned. I had to convince myself that I was breathing. Just for a moment. People on the street will tell you things if you stop and listen. I don't stop because I don't have any money.

THE FIRST TIME Lester Bangs listened to "Sister Ray" he could only hear the organ. Subsequent playings opened up whole sonic vistas he never knew were there. "Because properly conceived and handled noise is not noise at all."

EVERYTHING HAS BEEN written down. It's all around us. The rain fell in dashes; the air smelled metallic. I want to cross out every word I'm unhappy w/: ~~my job~~, ~~car trouble~~, ~~Oakland~~. I want to cross out everything that's left me waiting. ~~I want, I want, I want~~.... As if the sentence were a space where each word could thrive before wilting. As if this space were a sentence.

DAVID BOWIE'S EX-WIFE attempted suicide. His brother, Terry Jones, was successful. In an interview, Bowie spoke of his brother's tragic hanging. He was actually hit by a train.

PEOPLE STOOD BENEATH storefront awnings, eaves, newspapers, waiting out the rain. A feeling of community arose, a sense of renewal. But it passed. The water dried up. The news faded into the landscape, another tree in the distance. Throughout October, kids circled around the televisions in the university center watching CNN, wondering if the world would end. Nothing happened; everything changed.

MY FATHER PLAYING "Femme Fatale" for me on the way to school one morning. I don't know if I realized that the same band—without Nico—had created the impenetrable funk cacophony of "Sister Ray."

After seeing Oliver Stone's movie about the Doors at a friend's house, I asked my father why he hadn't told me that Nico was *so hot*.

"Oh," he shrugged, "Was she?"

THE FIRST TIME I took acid I could barely feel a change. Then I saw leaves arranging themselves into patterns, a reflection of the clouds. Something set the birds crashing. The sound was all we could see. I felt electricity in my eyes. Then the lights blew out on the streetcar. I was in love with everyone I saw. I was in love with electricity. Satellites make the television work. Later that year I vomited Robitussin out a streetcar window. Someone yelled, "That kid's puking blood!"

ROY BUCHANAN MADE several unsuccessful suicide attempts before hanging himself with his shirt in a police cell in 1988 following his arrest for drunk-driving.

WE WERE DISCUSSING baseball, how I don't understand how it can make anyone happy. But hope is only possible at the edge of the body. An entity of sound into which being enters. We were waiting for the never to arrive, to get some sleep. More likely you can't keep your nose out of those $50 baggies. She licked the glassine clean. To show us the world commerce created.

I'M EATING DINNER with a friend and his wife when the power goes out. We walk out onto the lawn. My friend's neighbors stand around, some drinking and laughing, as if the power outage were a sort of vacation. Or maybe they would be drinking and laughing anyway. I'm unable to think with the power out, as if a switch has been flipped inside my head. Then I remember that the power is still on in my neighborhood. I can think there. When it becomes apparent that the power won't come on soon, my friend and his wife go inside to find candles. I look around and it is still dark, so dark I cannot think.

Every day I wake up thinking, maybe I will do this for the rest of my life. After work, we make dinner, watch a movie then fall asleep. We dream we are sleeping next to each other.

America's in love with electricity. It's surging through our veins. There's nothing we can do but watch the cities go dark. The city is a body. Its skin is rust. I tried to disappear into it but came out material again. A year passed since I started writing this sentence. Could morning hold the light at bay? One afternoon all the snow was gone. A pause in nature's conversation with itself. This is all happening outside your window. As we speak. All possibilities are lost, a kite pulled across the water.

Nico viewed her beauty as a curse. Once her heroin addiction became all-consuming, she rarely bathed and let her teeth rot. Her son also became an addict. When he was lying in a hospital room in a drug-induced coma, she recorded the sounds of the life support machines for an album that she was working on.

THE LIGHTS WERE melting around us, trying to sleep. Adam asked me to take him to the hospital or call his mom—she would know what to do. I told him to try to sleep like the lights. Couldn't he see them? Anything moves faster when you stare at it. For a few moments, I felt like I was god. I could see life moving through everything. It's all made of water. This is what Whitman must've felt like, I thought. Then I never wanted to look at myself again.

IN THE FINAL scene of *Being There*, Peter Sellers walks out over the water, a visual metaphor for the willful suspension of disbelief. He buried himself in sentences. The motor's hum seeps in between notes. I've compiled the soundtrack to your life. It begins and ends in silence. The world becomes boring when you brush away the detritus. All we're left with is more numbers: zero one zero zero one one one one zero. They are collapsing around us.

I ONCE TRIED to write a poem called "My Father Was Sister Ray." I only had the title and tried to write my way out of it. I stopped after four lines:

> Before I put on my make-up
> I'm working to get to work
> working to get lost
> in someone else's body

That's as far as I got. I couldn't find the poem. Couldn't hit it sideways.

STRANDED UNDERWATER BETWEEN Oakland and San Francisco, the minutes recede in waves. I'm hours away from everything. Always already late. The minutes lose their color, until we can see through them into a future that is not ours. Soon we will carry it around as a memento, "the past." It floats beneath the words, a subtext. Don't worry, she's asleep. Do I mean for it to be this way—or am I just lazy? It kind of makes me sick, describing this nothingness, the way it stretches across the three rooms of our apartment. The way the rooms keep getting smaller each time we move. Space measured in dollars.

MARCEL DUCHAMP COMPRESSED a ball of twine between two square brass plates held in place by four long screws. He called this readymade *With Hidden Noise*. Duchamp had his friend Walter Arensberg place a small object inside the ball of twine without telling him what the object was. Thus the "hidden noise" can be heard when the readymade is shaken.

I WONDER IF my parents know about all the shit I did when I lived with them. Once I saw my dad's friend Frank in the parking lot of some punk show. It felt like the night was pressing needles into my skin. I kept rubbing my arms, pulling at my T-shirt. My pupils must have been as big as saucers. I think I was still 13. The show was held at a place for ex-addicts. They would always get mad if they caught you smoking pot there. It didn't matter if I was in love with anyone that night. My best friend and I stayed up laughing at pictures in our yearbook. I wish I still had it.

NICO DIED ON July 18, 1988 of a cerebral brain hemorrhage at the Cannes Nisto Hospital in Ibiza. She was taken to the hospital after being found lying unconscious beside her bicycle. She had quit using heroin two years earlier.

MY CHILDHOOD IS a song I can barely remember the words to. They only come back to me when I'm thinking of something else.

I could never write a memoir. My father bought me a purple Nerf frisbee made of soft rubber, the size of a personal pizza, limp as dough. My sister, Sarah, was upset because she wanted him to buy her something too, but he didn't have any money left. I didn't see him as much because I lived with our mother, and I think he just wanted to do something nice for me. I don't know why this makes me sad, now, almost 15 years later. The mind keeps its memories under glass.

EACH ARGUMENT BLOOMS like wild asphalt, all we see for miles. Vision is impaired or implied. Using the new headache system. But the body has a mind of its own. Especially at 2 a.m. with the radio on. Procession of Mission hipsters pedaling their track bikes into oblivion. They look half-dead and dynamite, pressed through pre-dawn dust. Each day is a mistake that you are tying around my neck. And we're coming to the chorus now.

RAY COMBS, HOST of the game show *Family Feud*, hanged himself with bed sheets in his hospital room while on a 72-hour suicide watch.

THE SCENE CHANGES. From rust to static, cloth to dust. Just like Sister Ray said. The sky darkened. I tasted aluminum in the back of my throat. I was afraid the side effects were taking shape. Everyone's afraid of something. I left work, walked out into Friday's dull static, my eyeballs fried from staring at the computer screen. I'd read a news story about a heavy metal guitarist who was shot on stage by a fan.

AT THE END of *Nashville*, after Ronee Blakley has been shot, Barbara Harris calms the crowd by singing "It Don't Worry Me." When she reaches the chorus, the crowd sings along in unison, "You may say that I ain't free, but it don't worry me." According to my father, that scene is a perfect metaphor for America. Once he found a poster of Ronee Blakley—a still from *Nashville*—in the garbage and gave it to me. Sometimes when I look at that picture I wonder, what has he ever given me? Something he found in the trash. The picture's framed, he repainted it, I shouldn't complain. I don't remember what I thought when he gave it to me. I was usually pissed at him, so who knows.

IN THE MEZZANINE's half-light, she looked all wrong, full of teeth. There'll probably be some music there, lining your eyelids. But we'll find a quiet place to talk. A bird folded into itself. Satellites are strangers. Out on the dark. A hospital blur of women that I will never speak to. Like junkies reading, more hip than a corpse. Who cares about Satie anymore anyway?

LOU REED AND John Cale both had affairs with Nico. Bob Dylan and Jackson Browne wrote songs for her. Maybe they too viewed her beauty as a curse. Cale produced Nico's first two albums, *Chelsea Girls* and *The Marble Index*. Lester Bangs wrote, "I don't know if I would classify it as oppressive or depressing, but I do know that *The Marble Index* scares the shit out of me."

I WILL NOT be allowed to love everybody. In high school I would fall in love with every woman I saw. The asphalt burned all day until the sky turned black. Smoke collects in the light above the pool table. You can't smoke anywhere anymore. Everything's already alight. Tomorrow we will walk through its ashes.

WHITE BARS OF light moved over the windshield, momentarily illuminating the interior of the car before turning dark again. The city tinted blue by the onset of night. For once I felt like I was living the life I wanted—a feeling I've rarely felt since. Later I recounted that night to her, the way the city looked as we listened to that song and how happy I felt. She just said, "That sounds so emo." I wished I hadn't said anything.

On December 9, 2005, former Pantera guitarist "Dimebag" Darrell Abbott was shot by a fan while performing with his band Damage Plan at a Columbus nightclub. A security guard, a club employee, and a concert attendee were also killed. Two others were injured.

I woke up hungover, my eye sockets filled with cotton. Walking to the 19th St. station, I couldn't see the rain, but I could feel it. The city was disintegrating. Some failed experiment. Everyone I passed looked damaged. A man asked if he could ask me a question. I didn't tell him that he already had—I just kept walking. He called me a coward motherfucker. Motherfuckin' coward. I hadn't been alone in months. The train was already ten minutes late. "By the time it gets here, it may as well've been the next one."

When I was in college, I looked all over the French Quarter for a copy of the *Nashville* soundtrack. It was reissued on CD a couple of years later. A girl that I had a crush on told me that a bookstore on Chartres St. had a copy for sale. She worked in a coffee shop, and I would stop in to talk to her on her breaks even though it was nowhere near anywhere I needed to go. Once she told me that when she was a kid, her mom would cry while playing solitaire and humming the theme song from *M*A*S*H**. I got the feeling she was an alcoholic. It took me all day to find the record. About a year later I saw a copy in a thrift store and bought it too.

You could only hope that describing the world would somehow change it. From water to ice and back again. After a few hours everything was darkened. It was all happening outside your reach. I can't shake the feeling that my name is in the back of someone's throat. A refrain repeating as I walk home in that post-work mindlessness: Now I have to start thinking again. Maybe that's what the guy pacing Grand Ave. tells himself or whomever he's talking to. Maybe he's making a catalog of his mistakes. Like this one.

Going to see some band play at the Mermaid Lounge and her stopping to kiss me in the abandoned lot where we'd parked. I still remember the exact wetness of her lips. The sound of cars from the overpass arcing through the night sky. Everything was so still. Knowing that moment was better than any rock show. Knowing no one could ever write a song about it.

SCENES AND CONVERSATIONS on the movie screen foreshorten reality. They are never coterminous with such moments in real life. That's why "real time" can feel so uncomfortable. As if the Earth had stopped dying for a moment. The sky pinned between trees. But we just kept dying anyway.

DARBY CRASH DIED of an intentional heroin overdose on November 7, 1980. He was 22 years old. The story goes that Darby entered into a suicide pact with a female friend. They bought $400 worth of heroin with Darby's earnings from a Germs reunion show. Darby injected his friend with a non-lethal dose and then injected enough heroin to kill himself four times over. In the morning the girl woke up next to Darby's dead body. Darby's older brother also died from an overdose.

YEARS LATER GERMS guitarist Pat Smear briefly played in another band whose lead singer would commit suicide.

"IF YOU ARE turned away by someone inscrutable whom you nonetheless love, what do you learn?" I don't know. *They want you or they don't.* Going to a party, and her insistence that I was *not* her boyfriend to anyone that asked. Not knowing if I've learned anything in my life, ever. Except that nothing is ever enough.

JOHN CAGE ENTERED an anechoic chamber at Harvard, expecting to hear pure silence. Instead he heard two sounds, one high and one low, caused by the whir of his nervous system and the blood pumping through his veins. The body is never silent. Maybe he rested his head on someone's chest. Damp grass touching my arm touching the skin beneath her t-shirt. I watch them floating; the stars quiver. "There is no such thing as empty space or time."

SOMEONE AT WORK asks me if I'm stoned. That morning I'd accidentally taken an extra antidepressant. I watch the conversation through a veil of gauze. Air the color of skin. Later that day, Jeff tells me a story about a friend who took an entire bottle of Prozac after eating half a sheet of acid. He tripped for two months then killed himself.

While touring Africa, Phil Ochs was attacked and strangled by robbers, damaging his singing voice, which lead to years of depression. He believed government agents had arranged the attack. After his death, it was revealed that the FBI had a 410-page file on Ochs.

Sometimes when I'd smoke hash everything around me would appear unbelievably clear—the opposite of being stoned. I felt that way on the train today. Everyone seemed to be made of glass. The air was empty. They all looked so alone. A girl was looking at her reflection in the window, adjusting her hair. I wondered how she could see herself. I couldn't read because I was moving backwards. I didn't want to anyway. I wanted to fall asleep and wind up at the airport, pretend like I was leaving town. I knew everyone would crowd onto the train once we crossed the bay. I shut my eyes and waited.

Walking back to the car I stopped and held her because I'd once heard a song about a couple dancing in a parking lot.

Toward the end of his life Phil Ochs talked constantly of suicide, joking about different ways he could kill himself. After an unsuccessful attempt in his apartment, Ochs hanged himself with a belt in his sister's suburban home. He waited until his nephew David—who eventually found Ochs's body—had gone next door to visit a friend.

A speck cut through a cloud above 8th and Franklin, a tear in the silver screen. Waiting to wait in line for two over rice—\$2.99, they never give you back the penny. When a white woman I work with orders in Mandarin, everyone behind the counter looks shocked. I just point at what I want.

A Chinese woman I work with also speaks Mandarin. She is always smiling. Today I passed her in the hall, and she said, "Andrew, you always smile." We only talk in hallways. I keep my address to myself. Everyone needs secrets at work.

I'D LIKE TO believe that Michael Hutchence accidentally hanged himself while trying to attempt autoerotic asphyxiation. More likely he intended to die.

SOMETHING FELL THROUGH my field of vision. My eyes like the sky, endless. Someone fell through the plot. Faye Dunaway, left out of focus, smolders. She looks tortured into shape, trapped in the motion of meaning.

THE LAST TIME I dropped acid, my next-door neighbor died. This really happened. After work one night, my friend Nolte and I decided to take these microdots that had been sitting in my freezer. It was a Saturday night. We didn't have anything else to do. I think we watched *Don't Look Back* on cable.

ON APRIL 24, 1975, Pete Ham, the lead singer of Badfinger, hanged himself in his garage studio in Surrey. His body was found by his girlfriend Anne Ferguson. Ham was almost penniless due to Badfinger's financial troubles, which he blamed on their manager Stan Polley. His suicide note read: "Anne, I love you. Blair, I love you. I will not be allowed to love and trust everybody. This is better. Pete. P.S. Stan Polley is a soulless bastard. I will take him with me."

Eight years later, Badfinger guitarist Tom Evans hanged himself in his garden.

I LIVED IN a fourplex in a pretty bad area of New Orleans that has since been gentrified. An elderly couple lived in the apartment next to mine. The only way I knew that anyone lived there was by the mail that would be in their mailbox when I got home from class and gone when I left for work.

ONCE IN WORKSHOP a friend of mine turned in a poem about selling microdots at a Sonic Youth concert. I think the poem ended with Kim Gordon taking her shirt off and something involving a hatchet. No one in the class knew what microdots were. I felt really lonely as I described what one looks like. No, it's much smaller than a sweet tart. I remember saying. Then walking home alone through snow. Already dark even though it was just after four.

WHY ARE SO many of these deaths by hanging? Doubtless there would be more overdoses than hangings if we consider them suicides—and they must be in some sense. Phil Lynott at some point must not have cared if he lived or died. Nick Drake's family never believed that he meant to kill himself. Due to his insomnia, Drake would often take an extra antidepressant to fall asleep at night.

HANK WILLIAMS WAS found dead of a drug overdose—a combination of heroin and alcohol—in the back of his hired car when his chauffeur was pulled over for speeding.

WHEN IT STARTED to get light out, I went back to my room to try to sleep. I left Nolte on the couch watching *The Simpsons.* Lying in bed, I watched multi-colored blocks arrange themselves in different patterns, like playing Tetris with my eyes closed. But my eyelids were made of sandpaper. I just wanted to get rid of my body for a few hours. You know that strychnine feeling when you can taste the electricity coursing through the air. And the only way to make it stop is to stay up until you're completely exhausted and then sleep for 16 hours.

Nothing in the air today. Nothing's worth waiting for. In the back of the cab, Dylan, head in hands. John Lennon shouts, "Pull yourself together, man! Chop chop money money!" You can feel that frustration inside each of us. Joan Baez in black and white sings "It's All Over Now, Baby Blue" beneath her breath in the back of another hired car. You can see her features so clearly, white leaves shining against a black lake. Each movement is made against a memory. Like Dylan in the movies.

1970: Janis Joplin, Jimi Hendrix overdose. 1971: Jim Morrison. They were each 27 years old.

The song "Lawns of Dawn" from *The Marble Index* was written after Nico took peyote with Jim Morrison in the California desert: "The light of the dawn was a very deep green and I believed I was upside down and the sky was the desert, which had become a garden and then the ocean. I do not swim and I was frightened when it was water and more resolved when it was land. I felt embraced by the sky-garden."

MORRISON'S WIDOW, PAMELA Courson, who some believe killed Jim by injecting him with a lethal dose of heroin, died three years later of an overdose. She was 27 years old.

NOLTE BANGING ON my bedroom door, saying the cops were coming up the stairs to my apartment. The stairs were on the outside of the building, large black ants rushing up them. But they weren't cops; they were paramedics. An ambulance was parked in the street with its lights flashing. At first I thought they were coming for me. Somehow the police knew I was dying and called the paramedics. Or maybe I had died and was watching all this happen outside myself like people say they do when they've had a near-death experience.

JOHN SIMON RITCHIE tried to kill himself multiple times after being arrested for the murder of his girlfriend Nancy Spungen. He was sent to Bellevue after trying to slit his wrists with a broken light bulb. Out on bail, he finally overdosed on heroin.

A few days after his cremation, Ritchie's mother found a note in his jacket pocket that read: "We had a death pact, and I have to keep my half of the bargain. Please bury me next to my baby in my leather jacket, jeans and motorcycle boots. Goodbye."

His mother claimed to have scattered his ashes over Spungen's grave.

ON DECEMBER 30, 1996, Jack Nance, star of *Eraserhead*, was found dead in his Pasadena apartment by a friend. He died of acute subdural hematoma caused by blows he'd sustained during an altercation with two men outside Winchell's donut shop the day before. Nance's health was failing due to years of drinking; he had joked that he would be easy to kill.

HOW COME SOMEBODY hasn't noticed that I'm dead and decided to bury me? God knows I'm ready. What she said. We watched the birds dive through smoke, feathers shining so brightly they seemed to be burning, like straight razors. I've been thinking of her as a ghost. Just another absence. Among the living and accessible.

THE PARAMEDICS WEREN'T coming to my apartment; they were going to the apartment next door. They brought out my elderly neighbor's body on a stretcher. But the stairway was pretty narrow, and they couldn't maneuver the stretcher down it. So the paramedics set the stretcher down right in front of my window. It looked like a dead body in a movie. His head seemed to be made out of wax. His mouth was open, gravity pulling his white hair back. Nolte and I sat on the couch with the television on, trying to act like nothing was happening. I kept thinking: that's a dead body, that's a dead body, that's a dead body....

Is it fitting that Nance died in such a Lynchian manner—involving a donut shop, no less? Did he die in the universe through which he entered the public consciousness? There are no suspects in the assault. Some believe it never happened, that it was just a story that Nance made up. An investigator on the case said that it is more likely that Nance—whose blood-alcohol level was .24 when he died—just got drunk and banged his head.

Billie Holiday was placed under arrest for heroin possession while on her deathbed. It was not heroin that killed her but cirrhosis of the liver caused by alcoholism.

THE PARAMEDICS FINALLY got my neighbor's body down the stairs, and the ambulance drove off. It felt like his body had been sitting there for hours. Nolte left without saying anything. I turned off the television and felt the silence pool around me. The sun was out. I was too scared to leave my apartment. After trying to sleep for an hour or so, I drove across town to my mom's house. I couldn't stop crying on the way over. In the rearview mirror my face looked like a ball of wax crushed by a fist.

I'M TIRED OF nothing happening, but it keeps happening all around us. Why not turn the other radio on? Pious hopes of the Red Sox clog the mind thoughtless. The curse has been reversed since I wrote that sentence. Everything I say is true if you believe it. I'm in love with Massachusetts, even though all its cities look alike—Northampton, Somerville, Gloucester covered in snow.

ON JULY 18, 1966, Bobby Fuller's body was found in a parked car near his Los Angeles Home. The death was ruled a suicide. Many people still believe Fuller was murdered.

MY MOM WAS working in her garden. It was now Sunday. I felt like someone scraped out my chest with a spoon. I was standing there holding my insides. I wanted my mom to tell me that I'd be all right. I wanted someone to tell me anything. I didn't know if I'd really seen my neighbor's dead body. I didn't know where I was. I'd just started my freshman year of college. A few weeks earlier, I lost my virginity to my roommate's girlfriend. I'd just turned 18.

JOHN BONHAM CHOKED on his own vomit.

CHRISTIAN MARCLAY RELEASED an album in 1985 called *Record Without a Cover*—which is what it was—a 12" black vinyl LP without a cover. The idea was that the vinyl would gather its inevitable abrasions from being unsheathed (an engraving on one side of the LP read DO NOT STORE IN A PROTECTIVE PACKAGE) and this would alter any subsequent playings.

I DON'T KNOW what it is about collecting things that makes it easier to be alone. It must have something to do with control. In high school I wouldn't talk to anyone who didn't listen to Black Flag. In college it was the Beach Boys. Maybe I wanted to own my aloneness. Shore up against it.

Tommy Dorsey, "The Sentimental Gentleman of Swing," choked on his own vomit.

Bupropion hydrochloride. Take 1 tablet orally daily for one week then 1 tablet orally twice daily. May cause drowsiness. Alcohol may intensify this effect. Use care when operating a car or dangerous machinery.

Everything happens to everyone. If not to you, then to someone you know. Your friend will get busted carrying works and forced into rehab. The next time you see him he'll be smoking crack in a cigarette outside The Saint. Your friend's best friend since forever will die of a heroin overdose before his 22nd birthday. Your roommate's little sister will be shot in the head during a drug deal. Barely past 20, she'll be the only one to survive, but she'll never see again. Maybe you'll start to write about these things. Or maybe you'll just start to think more and more about yourself. Maybe you won't be able to see any difference.

ON FEBRUARY 8, 1990, Del Shannon shot himself with a .22 caliber pistol. A year later, Shannon's wife filed a lawsuit against Eli Lilly & Co., the makers of Prozac, claiming the drug contributed to his suicide. Shannon had only been taking Prozac for 15 days.

AS YOU GROW older, some things become clear while others become clouded. I don't mind being poor, I just don't want to be a failure. I don't mind being a failure, I just don't want to be poor. Bon Scott graduated from being AC/DC's chauffer to being their lead singer, then choked on his own vomit.

WE DON'T WANT writers to tell us about their lives, we want them to show us something about *our own*. Maybe that's why I'm ashamed to tell you about my life. The irregular appearance of points on a surface. Maybe that's why no one talks about themselves in poems anymore. I was at a party and this guy kept interrupting himself, saying, "But me, me, me, it's all about me, anyway..." in an ironic, self-deprecating way. But he said it many times to different people so all night he really *was* talking only about himself. Maybe that's why we get tired of our own lives: they're all about us.

ON PALM SUNDAY of 1962 Clara Blandick, who played Auntie Em in *The Wizard of Oz*, took an overdose of sleeping tablets then pulled a plastic bag over her head.

I DON'T KNOW if I stopped taking acid because I stopped looking for it or if I just couldn't find any. In November of 2000, the DEA seized the largest operable LSD lab in agency history, arresting two men, Clyde Apperson and William Leonard Pickard. With this bust the DEA claims it reduced the LSD supply in the US by 95 percent. This claim has been widely disputed. On November 25, 2003, a federal judge sentenced Leonard Pickard and Clyde Apperson to life and 30 years, respectively.

WALKING OUT OF The Saint into early morning's underwater light. In the distance mist from the Mississippi rising above the barrier wall. Clothes strung across a clothesline. An undershirt shining, a slender dress. I could only think about leaving.

DONNY HATHAWAY JUMPED from the window of his 15th floor room in New York's Essex House Hotel.

LONELINESS ISN'T SOMETHING you feel. It's what you *are*. I am lonely. I am hungry. The car began to fill up at Embarcadero, by Montgomery it was packed. The people standing holding onto the overhead railing looked like they'd been hanged—heads bowed, eyes closed, their bodies swaying with the motion of the train.

YOU NEVER THINK to yourself, I will never feel this way again. You never know that this is the last time you'll have sex with her. That sentence only exists in the past tense. *That* time was the last. If you're ever stranded underwater between two cities, try to remember how it feels, so you can tell someone about it later, like a book you've read. Oh, what I would do for a good book to read on the train.

THE FIRST TIME I saw *Eraserhead* I was with my father. I was afraid that I might become Henry Spencer. That summer I stole a copy of *Blue Velvet* and watched it over and over. Years earlier my father and I religiously watched each episode of *Twin Peaks*. Sometimes my dad would imitate Jack Nance saying, "There's a fish in the percolator."

AFTER A THREE-MONTH prison stay for possession forced her to quit using heroin, Judee Sill started writing music. She was ashamed of her family's relative affluence—her stepfather was an animator for MGM studios—and was attracted to drug addiction and petty crime.

Sill felt uncomfortable playing before more established acts, and after a few abortive attempts opening for Graham Nash and David Crosby among others, she refused to do so, essentially ending her career.

I've been using my dictionaries as speaker stands. At night we crawl through our dreams. The buildings are wrapped in plastic. You were right about the end; it didn't make a difference. In sleep she claws at her dreams. Drunk, I slept through the film and awoke in an empty theatre.

Graham Nash heard rumors of Sill's death as early as 1974. She died of a drug overdose in November 1979. She was 35 years old. Some people believe that she died in Mexico. More likely, she was living in a trailer park in North Hollywood. An album from the year of her death, "Tulips from Amsterdam," is rumored to exist, and sometimes listed in her discography, but no one has heard it.

Any two things can fit next to each other. Just look at Jay-Z and *The White Album*. You see someone you think you know at a party but don't and then get to know her over a few months. This sameness in our experience can seem comforting. Everyone was talking to someone else. Each voice has been turned into a frequency. You just have to find it. I began to say something and wondered who was speaking. Like listening to my voice on the answering machine. Beep. Then silence between each statement of fact.

COMEDIAN FREDDY PRINZE's suicide note read: "I must end it. There's no hope left. I'll be at peace. No one had anything to do with this. My decision totally."

ALL SINGLE AND simultaneous sounds are given. Songs scattered across the landscape of the past. Listening to "Summer Babe" for the first time in a friend's car and thinking it was only noise. Later, alone in my room, I realized it was a California anthem. I'd never been to California.

I DO NOT operate a car or dangerous machinery regularly.

WRITTEN ON A wooden fence: SLAYER RULES, the "A" a rudimentary pentagram. The first time I heard Slayer I remember thinking Iron Maiden seemed so soothing in comparison. When you're a kid, "evil" actually means something. Metal as a genre exists to recapture that feeling.

IN 1973 SAMMY Davis, Jr. was inducted into the Church of Satan by Anton LaVey's daughter Karla.

THE PARAGRAPH IS an open field. At McKaren Park each blade of grass was glazed with ice. Across the field, VENM spray-painted on a brick wall in block letters. Short for "Venom," another metal band. Is this allusion what the author intended? Or should I say what the *artist* intended?

I CROSS THE street to the Turkey's Nest, which has just opened. Drink a beer in a 32oz. Styrofoam cup. Across the bar, an elderly woman talks quietly to herself. *It's been evening all day long.*

LISTENING TO "DJED" for the first time and in the middle, when the song breaks down into Atari static, I thought that my speakers were busted.

At a party, Alan Licht was surprised to hear a Herbie Hancock song playing. It was actually the first Tortoise record. That's when he knew the '80s were over.

ON JANUARY 31, 1954, Howard Armstrong, the inventor of FM radio, walked out a 13th floor window. He landed on a third story setback; his body wasn't discovered until the next day.

IN FEBRUARY OF 1969, after being arrested for marijuana possession in Texas, Roky Erickson pleaded insanity and was confined to Rusk State Hospital until the early '70s. He never recovered from the medication and electroshock treatments administered there, spending the rest of his life in and out of mental institutions.

DRIVING HOME FROM Tower Records listening to "The Portland Cement Factory at Monolith California," thinking, so this is what an acoustic guitar is supposed to sound like. (Tortoise took their name from John Fahey's publishing company.)

IN 1982 ERICKSON had a statement notarized claiming that he was inhabited by a Martian. A reporter from *Rolling Stone* found him living in a one bedroom house behind a porn store in Austin, where he would play a dozen sound systems simultaneously, "a rock station, gospel music, a police scanner or CB radio, a monster movie on the VCR, white noise."

EVERYONE WAS RUSHING to catch the last BART home. I felt like I was a part of something. The lights made the station look like a Van Gogh painting—you know that hazy glow around everything after you've been swimming. I made an effort not to sit too close to anyone on the train.

IN THE LATE '80s, beset by a series of medical problems, alcoholism and the dissolution of his second marriage, John Fahey was nearly destitute, living in a series of welfare motels and Salvation Army rooms in Salem, OR. He pawned his guitars and sold rare classical LPs that he found at local thrift shops to pay his rent. Even after he was rediscovered in the '90s, Fahey continued to live an itinerant life until his death by heart failure in 2001.

I NEVER KNEW you could lie in a poem. Then I realized you couldn't. I told myself that I wouldn't look back at what I'd written, but I'd written everything around me. The smoke like streams perched in the trees. They were made of verbs. I told myself I wouldn't look back. Light streams through smoke, a veil. No one can smoke in California. No one can breathe in California.

WE BUILD THESE little birds and hope that someone will buy them. A man standing by the side of the road in Arkansas sold flowers made from Coke cans. He made other things too, chairs and animals. We took them home and hoped they would soar. The sun cradles the city / before burning it down / once and for all. / She wanted to see everything at once. So she kept spinning. Our shadows were placed into the spaces the light left. Each moment is surrounded. I've kissed him before, I should know. I asked when the experiment would be over. Science is never finished. And so I keep writing.

SAM COOKE WAS shot to death by Bertha Franklin, manager of the Hacienda Motel, where he was staying. Franklin claimed that she killed Cooke in self-defense after he raped a young woman then threatened Franklin. His death was ruled justifiable homicide.

THERE ARE MOMENTS when I listen to John Fahey records and I feel closer to those sounds than all the times someone I love has said my name. Once she began a sentence with "Andrew" and I realized she hadn't said my name since the night we met. I don't remember that night, only her saying my name. In the book I'm reading, the man the narrator is in love with says her name, but the author does not write the name, only "And then he said my name." I know exactly how she—the narrator and the author—felt.

THE MOST MUNDANE conversation becomes illuminating when recorded. That's the premise of Francis Ford Coppola's film *The Conversation*. That's the beauty of found sound. Beneath each sound there is a story. The plot beats like a heart. Cries connect each circumstance. Lines between crows between telephone poles. I was talking just to feel the words in my mouth.

STEVEN PAUL SMITH's body was found in the kitchen of his girlfriend's Los Angeles home with two knife wounds to the chest. *A little less than a suicide.* "I'm sorry—love, Elliot. God forgive me" was written on a post-it note found near his body. It is unclear whether the name "Elliott" was misspelled in the note or by the coroner. Smith had attempted suicide at least once previously. Toward the end of his life he had been known to use heroin and crack cocaine, but no drugs or alcohol were present in his system when he died.

WALKING OUT OF the house, it was colder than I'd thought, so I went back inside and put on a jacket. I was hot walking home, so I took my jacket off. Things like that happen to me every day.

LATELY THE SOUNDTRACK to the city has become whatever I can get my hands on. Dust embedded in the black turns its sound into something we can see. I can't listen to music that often. The record lives on as an entity unto itself. Gray cloud banks with lights of Oakland shining beneath. The train's heart murmur. The night was all around us. Schoenberg sent everyone to the blackboard. Here's your chance to make me feel awkward. The light kissed her skinny throat. Waves lapping at the foot of our bed.

IN 1976 JACK Goldstein began producing a series of audio works, the first of which was a suite of nine 45 rpm 7-inch records of sound effects. The records were paired with titles suggestive of their audio content and pressed in colored vinyl visually related to the sounds. For example, *The Tornado* was pressed on purple vinyl because Goldstein observed that purple was the color of tornadoes when photographed. *The Dying Wind* was pressed on clear vinyl. On March 14, 2003, Goldstein hanged himself from a tree outside his mobile home in San Bernardino, CA.

WE ARE A long way from a pop song. The dynamics are exceptionally low, but audible. No one has a story anymore, now that everything's being recorded. I am sitting in a stranger's living room watching television when someone says "Andy," and for a moment I don't know to whom he is referring. Thin film of dust over the screen. Then there is the feeling I get in any large city that there is no reason for anyone to speak to me. What would I have to say? No one has a story to tell. I'm saving up these thoughts to fill the clouds above our heads. I'm saving myself from misinterpretation.

EACH BILLBOARD IS a monument to our ability to believe in anything, at least for a moment. Then it's gone. Light floods the airshaft, each window's white falling into dust. I wouldn't have written about it if I hadn't seen it. Everyone's talking about the weather. Whole channels are devoted to it. Snow makes all cities look alike, obscuring whatever nature is left. And a city is nothing but nature. What's more natural than a 7-11's storm and stress?

GRAM PARSONS OVERDOSED in a room at the Joshua Tree Inn. His road manager Phil Kaufman and a friend, Michael Martin, got very drunk, borrowed a broken down hearse and drove to LAX to retrieve the body, which was being prepaired to be flown to Louisiana for burial. Following Gram's wishes, they set his body ablaze in the desert. The two were arrested several days later and fined $700 for stealing and burning the coffin—it was not against California law to steal a dead body.

RIDING MY BIKE home drunk from a party, I wake up in the emergency room. A doctor tells me that I have a subarachnoid hemorrhage. My brain was bleeding, but it stopped. They are just holding me for observation. To make sure the swelling goes down. A week later I turn 26.

I'M DISCHARGED FROM the hospital and catch a cab home. I'm afraid that I will receive a ticket for biking while intoxicated or for riding a bike without brakes. At the police station, a cop gives me back my bike without saying a word. For weeks I'm afraid I'll receive a summons or a ticket in the mail. All I get are bills from SF General for a CAT scan and from the fire department for the ambulance ride, which I forward to my insurance company. Two weeks later I lose my coverage when I quit my job. All told, I owe SF General $50.

KEITH MOON OVERDOSED on Heminevrin, an anti-seizure medication he was taking to wean himself off alcohol. The flat that he died in had been loaned to him by Harry Nilsson. A few years earlier, Mama Cass died in the same bed in the same room of heart failure (not, as rumor would have it, from choking on a ham sandwich). Distraught over these two deaths, Nilsson sold the flat to his friend Pete Townshend.

EVERY TIME I stand up I get lightheaded and stumble. On my birthday I drink a vodka tonic and get so dizzy I can't stand. Later that night I drink a beer and feel fine. I'm relieved that I can start drinking again. My last birthday in San Francisco. Whatever doesn't kill you makes you dizzy.

DON'T YOU WONDER sometimes about sound and vision? "The birds there above the lake sound the way the lights look." The lights strung above the water were alight, black wire connecting each to the next. The way thinking of you connects me to you. The way thinking I'm Jesus makes me Jesus. For a moment at least. A bird was bathing near the curb. The current carries trash toward a sewer grate. EMPTIES INTO THE BAY. Each thought was straining to be thought through one Percocet, one Valium, pseudoephedrine, two Heinekens. Each pill is a pep talk. The light emptied into the water. The sky darkened. I tasted aluminum rising in my throat.

THERE ARE TIMES when talking to someone in a bar and you can only see her mouth. You're telling her things you would never tell someone you know. Too drunk to hide. Not what you're thinking. You are afraid that your mother is dying. If my mother dies, I will be totally alone. Her mother died three years ago—of the same type of cancer that your mother has.

And all I can think is: why does she have to have a boyfriend? How can you keep living when no one knows you are there? Her father is dead too, she told you. Her voice drowned out by the jukebox. She is 22, three years younger than you.

IN LATE DECEMBER 1983, just after his 39th birthday, Dennis Wilson drowned while drunk.

AND WHY AS she talks do you just want to kiss her? It is almost 2 a.m. I can't remember my name. She says she's an alcoholic. She wears it well. A weak smile. Lips too red, slight gap between her front teeth.

AT SOME POINT your life becomes a b-side. You're just singing along. "Lookin' for a party, some action." The city loops back onto itself like a memory. That's beside the point. I can't tell if I'm remembering something that already happened or if I'm dreaming. To be lost can become a relief. To be purposeless, to be implausible. I've spent most of my life trying to make up my mind.

I swear I saw a New Orleans streetcar riding down Church Street the other day, "Desire" printed above the driver's window.

FROM NEW ORLEANS to Missoula. I'd never walked through snow before. From Missoula to Oakland. I never wanted to see snow again. From Oakland to San Francisco. Waking up to move the car to the other side of the street. From San Francisco to Albany. The day before Thanksgiving, snow was just starting to fall as I left. From Albany to Brooklyn. There is no snow in Brooklyn, only piles of dirt flecked white.

FOR THE FIRST time in months, no one told me what to do today. So I skimmed over the hours like a paragraph without punctuation. Joe gave me a handful of Xanax. I will save them for a day that is less hopeless. Tomorrow, maybe.

TRAFFIC IS A tone poem to a city planner. Van Ness to Mission is only a line about love and death. Its iambic lurch connecting two ideas I've never thought before and won't remember because I don't have anything to write with. Every other block, another ping means a stop has been requested. The loneliest sound I've ever heard until I step off the bus and hear a woman singing softly to herself in Spanish. Glass scattered across the sidewalk shimmers beneath Doc's Clock's neon north star.

JOHNNY THUNDERS DIED of methadone and alcohol poisoning in New Orleans—my hometown—in 1991. He was 38 years old.

EACH STATEMENT IS a fact. The memoirist is a liar. These swords hurt my throat. I tried to write a poem called "Wealth Distribution." The first line was, "Every morning I wake up eating my own face"—I had been reading the Clark Coolidge book *Own Face*. Every morning my breakfast is handed to me in a paper bag. With extra hot sauce.

I LIGHT UP in the alley behind MacArthur station and can't tell if it's raining or if I'm just sweating. As in *Music for 18 Musicians* the changes accumulate slowly until everything has changed. That's the power of the radio's endless epiphanies, everyone can relate. A quiet love is better than none. We were waiting for the light to die behind the clouds' eyelids. The eye is an association of everything we've seen. I saw veins pulsing, shifting in place.

ON NOVEMBER 7, 1987, John William Mister took an overdose of antidepressants then called his ex-wife on the telephone before passing out unconscious. When she arrived at his house the paramedics were lifting him into the ambulance. He spent the next week in a psychiatric hospital.

THE DAY MAKES its noise and we all listen. The sky's the color of urine, the color of the spine of Robert Creeley's *Collected Poems*.

I still don't know what silence equals. You keep insisting that I have something to tell you. Each channel is a reflection of someone's thoughts. I can't understand a thing. Each television screen is a point in a constellation we're sewing together in our sleep.

LIFE IS OTHER than what one writes. Not many authors haunting these pages. Is it of any significance that John Berryman committed suicide by jumping into the river I grew up not three miles from? Though 1,300 miles away. His youngest daughter was just six months old. Anything becomes significant when you stare at it long enough. Berryman's father also committed suicide.

MIDNIGHT CAME AND went in an hour. Some trains have no discernible schedule. Water moves between the tracks like the scales of a snake. A rat nudges a Duracell battery with its nose. CAUTION: Rodenticide. All you can do is wait. Everyone's waiting for something. Nothing changed. No one looks at one another on the platform. I walk out of the station into early morning's milky light.

I'VE TRANSCRIBED THIS argument with myself. Everyone can relate. Especially at 2 a.m. with the radio between stations. Under the moonlight, the serious moonlight. He was trying to let the sky into an empty room. Like the one you're sitting in now. In the year of the medicated. I wanted the white space to bleed into words before you started crossing them out. To dissolve each distance in distance. I should've just shut the fuck up. That's the story of my life. Everyone can relate.

IS IT POSSIBLE to have never had a father? Growing up, sometimes I felt like Jesus: my father was a ghost. I have a friend who's never met his father. He knows his name, what city he lives in. Maybe he feels like some piece of himself he's never known but can feel is lost in that city. A piece of my father died when he didn't—that part of him that would not live for me.

AN APPEAL TO rock and roll will tell us almost nothing worth knowing. I know what it feels like to need a specific person, but I can't say what need *is*. I'd like to tell you how death infects our lives, how we are all living with it, but I can only relate how Johnny Ace died.

I've been so depressed lately. I've never read that line in a poem. I'd rather some attempt at beauty. Is anything beautiful anymore anyway? The light that drains through the tracks of the JMZ, a malt liquor halo. Every day I walk through it on my way home from work. On my way out of sleep.

Some sources say Johnny Ace died playing Russian roulette, others believe it was a mob hit. Lou Reed wore a white armband to school the day after his death.

Brian Jones drowned under the influence of alcohol and sedatives. The coroner's report stated the cause as "death by misadventure." A builder who had been renovating Jones's house at the time is said to have confessed to the murder on his deathbed.

In grad school I wrote this poem about my dad trying to kill himself. I think the first line was "My father in the back of the ambulance asks for his cigarettes." It was supposed to be kind of a joke. I wanted to laugh it off. Scotch tape over it with words that weren't mine. No one really cared either way. It was easier if they just didn't get the joke.

I MISS THE ice hanging from gutters in the alley behind my apartment. Wind lifted snow into the light from a streetlamp. I just stood there. Everything was crisp as a photograph. A year later, I was gone. When I was in high school I felt like I missed a friend I'd never known. It was around that time that I read about Elvis's twin brother who died shortly after he was born. I don't know where I read that or if it's true.

SKIP SPENCE WAS declared dead of a drug overdose by a coroner in Santa Cruz, only to get up and ask for a glass of water.

IS THERE ANYTHING left to talk about? The night spread out like wax. In the bathroom of the Turkey's Nest, I pulled my dinner from my pocket. I pressed my fingers through the faucet's tarnished gold. And then the strings came in.

SOMETIMES MY DAD would wear the scrubs that he'd been given as an inpatient around the house. In the poem he's wearing them as we play football on the front lawn. I didn't really remember that scene, just the feeling that someone knew. I wondered why he didn't get rid of the evidence: the scrubs, the hospital bracelet he kept in his dresser drawer like a badge. I think I even used that metaphor. When my mom got to his house, the paramedics were lifting him into the ambulance, and he asked her for his cigarettes. She told me about it years later.

FAILURE IS IN the eyes of the beholder. Each listener must imagine what *Smile* might have sounded like had it been completed. It is pure possibility, the Platonic ideal of a pop record.

SOMEONE MISSES YOU. It is beautiful here. When I was in college I would sometimes go days without talking to anyone. I was slowly disappearing. I had to remember to breathe. Maybe that's why I want to tell people these things, people I will never know. Walking down Montgomery toward North Beach, no one would look at me. I wondered if I was even there. I felt the air touching my skin. It felt human. If I don't leave my apartment nothing will happen. Nothing ever happens anyway.

George Eastman's suicide note read: "To my friends: my work is done. Why wait?"

Joy wants everything to remain eternally the same. Maybe that's what Nico found in a life devoted to procuring heroin. Will music ever mean anything to me again, or will songs only remind me of the first time I heard them? Maybe that's what Judee Sill felt wasting away in a trailer in North Hollywood. Maybe that's what John Fahey asked himself lying in bed in a welfare motel listening to a record of Gen. Douglas MacArthur's farewell speech. Maybe they just stopped and didn't think about it.

"Don't worry, it's not loaded." Said Terry Kath, guitarist and co-founder of Chicago, before shooting himself while playing Russian roulette.

Lunch trumps ambition every time. At the diner, our waitress described Wednesday's specials in hushed tones. We were eating out of her hands. I thought she said, "nothing will ever make this stop." Everyone laughed when Joe ordered spaghetti and meatballs.

THE POEM WAS about my French tutor. About the time she told me that her mother committed suicide. I tried to pantomime my boredom with one of her lessons by putting my index and middle fingers into my mouth, thumb cocked back then released. I looked up at the kitchen ceiling. Then she told me. I wanted to tell her about my father. But I realized that there's a hierarchy to grief. Her mother was dead, my father wasn't. Another time she accused me of being stoned during our lesson. I wasn't stoned, I was just really hungry.

"I DON'T BELIEVE that people should take their own lives without deep and thoughtful reflection over a considerable period of time," read the suicide note of Wendy O. Williams, who rose to fame singing almost naked with strategically placed pieces of duct tape as the front woman for The Plasmatics.

MY GIRLFRIEND WALKS to work over the Williamsburg Bridge during the transit strike. I lie in bed and feel each point where our bodies touched while we slept. The highest paid MTA employees make about $53,000 a year. There are plenty of ways to know you're not dying. Whatever light is left in the sky when she gets out of work.

IN ALL THE pictures I have of my father, he looks so unhappy. Sitting there wearing a too-tight T-shirt from the Audubon Zoo, holding me and my sister in his lap. I can't remember my parents ever being together. They are always in separate houses. In his driver's license photo my father's eyes are closed. It's the flash that does it. I always got a kick out of that. I don't know why the people at the DMV didn't make him retake it. Maybe they did and he just closed his eyes again.

Andy Mister is a writer and artist. He attended Loyola University and the University of Montana. His writing has appeared in *Boston Review*, *Colorado Review*, *Fence*, *Northwest Review*, *Verse*, and many other journals. He is the author of the chapbook *Hotels* (Fewer & Further, 2007). Born in New Orleans, he lives and works in Brooklyn, NY.

CPSIA information can be obtained at www.ICGtesting.com
Printed in the USA
LVOW11s1213211013

357812LV00001B/8/P